Wiccan Spells for Beginners

The ultimate guide to Wicca and Wiccan spells for health, wealth, relationships, and more!

Table Of Contents

Introduction 1

Chapter 1: Spells for Different Lunar Stages 2

Chapter 2: Tools and Equipment for Rituals and Ceremonies 5

Chapter 3: Using Ingredients for Spells 11

Chapter 4: How to Cast a Spell 14

Chapter 5: Spells and Days of the Week 16

Chapter 6: Truth Spells on a Sunday 20

Chapter 7: Spells to Boost Confidence on a Monday 22

Chapter 8: A Protection Spell on a Tuesday 25

Chapter 9: A Spell to Improve Communication on a Wednesday 26

Chapter 10: A Money Spell on a Thursday 27

Chapter 11: A Love Spell on a Friday 28

Chapter 12: A Binding Spell on a Saturday 29

Conclusion 30

Introduction

I want to thank you and congratulate you for downloading the book, "Wiccan Spells for Beginners".

This book contains helpful information about Wicca, what it is, and how you can use Wiccan spells for a range of uses.

This guide is ideal for beginners to Wicca, who are looking for some simple spells to try out.

You will be provided with information on how to create your own spells and chants, along with the best days and times to perform particular spells. You will also be given a list of sample spells that you can try out, that are simple enough for any beginner to master.

This book will explain to you tips and techniques that will allow you to successfully understand and use Wiccan magic from home. You'll learn about how Wicca works, along with the tools necessary for performing Wiccan magick effectively.

Getting accustomed to using Wiccan magick properly can take some time, but with the help of this book you'll be well on your way to mastering some simple Wiccan spells fast!

Thanks again for downloading this book, I hope you enjoy it!

Chapter 1:
Spells for Different Lunar Stages

Wicca is a religion that involves spells and rituals. It also involves god and goddess worship. If you have just been initiated into a Wiccan group, learning how to cast spells should be a major focus. However, as a beginner, you should opt for spells that are simple and easy to cast. Since you have not yet mastered spell-casting, you should not try to dabble with complicated spells that require ingredients that are hard to find.

Also, you have to learn how to meditate, visualize, and bring yourself into a trance. You need to have a clear mind when casting a spell. You should not have scattered thoughts, so that you can effectively send out your desires to the universe. Keep in mind that casting a spell is communicating with the universe. If you do not want to send mixed signals, you must learn how to control your mind.

Spells and Phases of the Moon

You may wonder if certain spells work better during certain moon phases. For most Wiccan traditions, the cycles of the moon are crucial in their magickal works. They believe that the waxing moon, the waning moon, the new moon, and the full moon possess special magickal properties, which is why their spells have to be planned accordingly.

During the waxing moon, for instance, spells for love, inspiration, friendship, freedom, happiness, and prosperity are ideal. Positive magick or magick that draws things to you is commonly performed. The moon grows from dark to full within about fourteen days. So if you want to cast a spell to bring love into your life, give you a promotion at work, or make you more financially independent, you better do it at this time.

During the waning moon, the moon turns from full to dark within about fourteen days. Most Pagan and Wiccan traditions perform baneful magick or magick that gets rid of, destroys, or sends away things that they no longer want in their life at this time. The waning moon is actually the perfect time to cast spells against addictions and negative powers. It is also ideal for breaking curses and banishing bad habits.

If you want to end a relationship, eliminate toxic people from your life, or reduce negative things such as debts and health problems, you should cast such spells during the waning moon. It is also the perfect time to perform a rite to get rid of hostile influences in your life.

The new moon, on the other hand, is the most ideal time to cast spells for love, romance, health, work, and new beginnings. It is during this phase that the moon becomes dark before waxing once again after it has waned for three days. However, you may find it quite difficult to see the moon during this time. It may appear as a faint crescent of silver low in the sky.

In addition, many Wiccan traditions consider this time as a fallow time wherein individuals are expected to rest and rejuvenate before they begin to work on more intense magickal workings. Other traditions, however, consider this time as the best time to perform magick related to wish fulfillment as well as mind and body purification, sacred space, and magick related to peace and inner harmony.

Finally, there is the full moon. It is during this time when you are able to see the whole side of the moon. Many Pagan and

Wiccan traditions perform magickal workings on the full moon, the day before it, and the day after it. So for a total of three days, they perform rituals that are focused on spiritual development and personal growth. You can use this time to cast spells for healing, intuitive awareness, wishes, predictions, and better relationship with the deities.

Chapter 2:
Tools and Equipment for Rituals and Ceremonies

Pagan, Wiccan, and other traditions use a variety of tools for their elaborate ceremonies and rituals. They use specific items for casting spells and drawing circles. Since you are a modern practitioner, you can use contemporary items or other things that can serve as substitutes if you cannot get hold of ancient tools.

For your altar, you should have all or some of the following tools. The altar is a very important element in ceremonies and rituals. Your altar can be a simple table or an elaborate customized altar.

Wand

You can purchase a wand from a magic store or have one customized with engravings. Generally, your wand should complement the length of your fingers, hand, and elbows, but it is still up to you how long you want it to be. You can also choose any material for your wand, but most witches go for those made from wood.

Sword and Athame

Both the sword and the athame are sharp tools that can be used for carving or cutting ingredients and other items necessary for spells, rituals, or ceremonies. An athame is a short wooden knife that largely resembles a dagger. It is smaller than a sword, which comes in different shapes and sizes. Most witches choose a double-edged wooden athame.

Boline

It is another sharp tool that is used for cutting sacred items during rituals and ceremonies. It is actually a short knife with a curved blade and a white handle.

Besom

It is a broom that is used during the cleaning part of a ritual. When using your besom, you do not have to literally sweep the floor. You can use it to sweep around in a symbolic manner. Witches generally choose a besom that is made with natural materials. They either purchase one or make their own, following the guidelines of their tradition.

Bell

A bell is used to invoke deity and attract positive energies. You can choose a bell of any size or shape, although you may want to choose a small one for easy handling.

Chalice

It is a cup with a long stem and resembles a wine glass. It is used to contain the wine or fruit juice necessary for the ritual or ceremony. You can use a chalice made from glass, brass, or any other material.

Cauldron

It is basically an iron pot with a huge bottom and three legs. It is used to contain the ingredients you need for your ritual or ceremony.

Crystal Ball

It is a ball used to have a vision of the past, present, or future. It represents the Goddess and has long been used in witchcraft and similar practices.

Sensor

It comes in different shapes, sizes, and materials, although it is typically made with brass. It is used to hold burning incense to disperse smoke during rituals and ceremonies.

In Wicca, gods and goddess from different traditions, including the Celtics, Egyptians, Romans, and Greeks are usually called upon. So those who practice Egyptian magick use the following tools and equipment for their rites:

Flail and Crook

A flail is used as a wand for magickal rituals while a crook is similar to the staff of a shepherd.

Djed Pillar

It symbolizes stability and looks like a short pillar with four platforms. The Djed is actually the phallus of the god of the Tree of Life.

Ankh

It symbolizes life, energy, creative power, and unlimited fertility. It is basically an Ansata cross with a piece of sandal strap. The vertical and horizontal bars of its lower tau cross section represent the masculine and feminine energies. On the other hand, the top part of its loop represents the power of the sun as well as rebirth and reincarnation.

Staff or Scepter

It is basically a staff that is made with a dried bull's penis. It represents domination and power.

Scarab

It is the symbol of Ra, the god of the sun. It is actually a beetle that transforms from being an egg into an adult. Its movement in the dung are comparable to the movement of the sun in the sky. Its colorful wings are also comparable to the day and night. In essence, it is an amulet that is worn for protection.

Lotus Flower

It is also referred to as Sensen. It represents the sun, reincarnation, and creation. It has long been used by the ancient Egyptians in their magickal rituals. Likewise, it was considered a holy flower by the ancient Indians.

Buckle of Isis

It is also called the Blood of Isis and the Knot of Isis. It is basically a funerary amulet that is made from colored glass or red stone. It is believed to be used by the gods of ancient Egypt for eternal life and resurrection. It is also associated with the goddesses Nut, Nephtys, and Hathor.

Sistrum

It is a sacred musical instrument from the percussion family and is used in royal courts for conducting spiritual and religious ceremonies as well as dancing while honoring the goddess Hathor. It is believed to unleash powers that can drive away Set, the storm god. It is also held by Bast, a goddess of joy, happiness, dance, festivity, and glad tidings.

Eye of Horus

It was originally called the Eye of Ra. Ancient Egyptians believed it to possess the powers of reincarnation and rebirth. It represents courage, protection, and royal power.

Maat's Feather

It is actually an ostrich feather that is used for magickal ceremonies. However, if you have difficulty acquiring one, you can use a peacock feather as a substitute.

Uraeus

It is the spitting cobra of Africa. It represents royalty, sovereignty, aristocracy, deity, divinity, and freedom in ancient Egypt.

Amulet

It is an ornament or object made from a variety of substances and materials. It was originally used by the ancient Egyptians to protect their soul and body against bad spirits, evil gods, ill omens, and ghosts. It can have any design or style, as long as it signifies supernatural powers.

Nemes

In ancient Egypt, pharaohs wore nemes or striped head cloths to cover their heads and protect against the heat of the sun.

Gold and Other Precious Stones

For the ancient Egyptians, gold was likened to the skin of the gods while silver was to their bones. Precious stones, such as lapis lazuli were also used to represent the gods and goddesses.

Numbers and Knots

Knots symbolize the convergence of the forces of nature while numbers represent the abstraction of knots. The number seven is actually highly significant in Egyptian mythology for it is believed to possess compelling powers.

Letters to the Dead

The ancient Egyptians used to write letters to departed friends and relatives for forgiveness, help, and counseling.

Wax Figures

These are objects used to represent immense anger and hatred.

Lamp

During a ritual or ceremony, you can use a lamp or any special type of light source to represent the evil and good forces of nature.

Chapter 3:
Using Ingredients for Spells

When casting a spell, potions are frequently used. You can make a potion using a variety of ingredients such as herbs and essential oils. Make sure that you use the right ingredients so that your potions will work. Also, see to it that you handle the ingredients with care.

Some of them may be toxic and not advised to be ingested or handled with bare hands. For added safety, you should do your research about the ingredients that you need before you use them. Nonetheless, here are some of the most common ingredients used for spell-casting and making potions.

- Basil is typically used for exorcism purposes, but it can also be used for love spells and protection spells. This herb represents a healthy mind and body. Hence, it can also be used to prevent nightmares and counter bad dreams with good ones. Caraway seeds are also used in spells to achieve a sound mind and body. They can also be used to enhance memories and have a sharper mind for exams.

- Bay leaves are believed to have the ability to predict the future and help with psychic readings. They are usually used in potions for healing and improving overall health. Anise is very important and is actually a must-have in protection potions. It is said to help purify the soul so a person can seek the goodness in life and stop worrying about any negative forces that may bring them down.

- Coriander is typically used in healing potions to alleviate sickness. Nonetheless, it can also be used to enhance the powers of love potions. It is said to have the ability to draw a certain person into another. Because of this, it is commonly used by people who want to use love potions in their spells.

- ➢ Garlic cloves, on the other hand, are used in potions to drive away evil spirits and obtain protection against sickness and pains. However, it can also be used for love spells and money spells.

What If You Do Not Have Any Ingredients?

While some ancient spells require ingredients that are hard to find, modern versions of these spells can be done using simple ingredients from your kitchen. There is no more need for you to gather ingredients from a forest or sacrifice animals. Modern witches are more practical. You can just go to your local market to purchase the ingredients that you need. In fact, you can even cast spells without using any ingredients.

For instance, you can cast a love spell with only your mental ability. Even though you do not have any herbs or essential oils, you can create an effective spell by using your intuition, concentrating, and visualizing your desired outcome. If you are doing your ritual in your garden or yard, you can use the elements around you.

You can pick up a rock or a stone and incorporate it into your ritual. You can also use sand or water. Whatever element you use, make sure that you charge it with the intention of turning it into the tool that you need. Keep in mind that visualization and intuition are the key for casting spells without ingredients.

Let us say that you want to do a love spell but you do not have any ingredients on hand. What should you do in this case?

Well, you should go on with the steps of casting a spell as usual; but instead of using ingredients, you should focus on the qualities that you want your potential partner to have.

It is not advisable to focus on a particular person because that will be against the rules of Wicca. When casting a spell, you have to make sure that you do not hurt or take away the free will of another person. If you want to draw love into your life, you should focus on the qualities that you want to attract and not a specific person.

You should meditate, visualize, and raise your energies. You also have to be very clear about your intentions. If you do not want to forget anything, you should write down your spell or chant on a piece of paper. While you can use a spell made by someone else, it is better to use your own.

If you want your love spell to work more efficiently, you should continue doing it for several months. This way, you can harness your magickal powers better by practicing visualizations daily. Even if you do not have any ingredients, you can light candles, if you have any, during your rituals.

Chapter 4:
How to Cast a Spell

In general, rituals are performed by casting a circle, stating your purpose, invoking the deities, performing magick, and closing the circle respectively. While you can perform a short or long ritual that involves various tools and ingredients, you have to follow the basic steps of how to cast a spell.

First of all, you need to cast a circle to open up the portals and allow spirits to be present during your ritual. You can do this by using your wand or simply by walking around three times. When casting a circle, you need to start from the North and move in a clockwise direction.

After that, you need to state your purpose clearly and precisely. As much as possible, you should state what you want in a loud and commanding voice. You can have as many requests as you want, but it is ideal to focus on just one for every ritual. Also, you may want to write down the details of your request, so you will not forget them.

When that is done, you should call upon the gods and goddesses of your choice. There are deities that represent various aspects, such as health, love, and protection. Make sure that you do research on these deities so you can successfully call upon the right one during your rituals.

You can invoke Aphrodite, for instance, if you are doing a love spell. You can request for her presence in the form of an apparition or ask her to enter your body. In addition, see to it that you brought the correct type of offering if you have any. Once you have invoked the deities, you can start performing magick.

See to it that you tell the god or goddess your desires and ask him or her to help you achieve them. Make sure that you focus all your energy on what you truly desire. When you are done speaking to the deity, you should thank him or her and give your offering. You can give a generic offering such as wine, milk, or fruit juice.

Finally, you need to close the circle by re-tracing it using your wand or walking in a counter-clockwise direction three times. This step is crucial as it is meant to close the portal that you have opened. After you cast your spell, you have to free the energies and deities that you have called upon.

Chapter 5:
Spells and Days of the Week

In many Wiccan and Pagan traditions, the days of the week are significant for casting spells. So if you are planning to cast a certain type of spell, make sure that you do it on the right day.

Each day of the week is actually associated with a specific planet as well as colors, deities, and elements. While you can cast a spell anytime and any day you want, you can have a higher chance of being successful with it if you cast it on the right day.

- ➢ On Sundays, you should cast truth spells and spells that generate warmth in your heart. Sunday is represented by the Sun and the deities Ra, Brighid, and Helios. So if you feel frigid and resentful, you should use the energy of the sun to take away the anger and resentment in your heart.

    Sunday is also represented by gold, diamond, quartz crystal, amber, and carnelian, as well as marigold, cinnamon, and sunflower. It is also associated with beauty, agriculture, hope, creativity, victory, and self-expression.

- ➢ On Mondays, you should cast spells that are powered by your emotions. Monday is the best day to cast a spell for improving intuition and increasing confidence. It is also perfect for casting spells for protection and clairvoyance. This day is represented by the colors white, silver, and light blue.

    Monday is also ruled by the moon and represented by the deities Thoth and Selene. Moreover, it is represented by silver, pearl, moonstone, and opal, as well as catnip, sage, chamomile, comfrey, wintergreen, and other mints. It is also associated with childbearing, family life, purity, virginity, wisdom, healing, and intuition.

- On Tuesdays, you should cast spells that inspire energy and passion, as well as increase your confidence. You should cast spells that can help you win a spiritual battle. Tuesdays are also great for casting protection spells.

Tuesday is actually ruled by the planet Mars and is represented by the deities Mars, Lilith, and Aries. It is also represented by the colors orange and red, as well as holly, cactus, coneflower, and thistles. Tuesday is associated with iron, garnet, and ruby. It is also linked to conflict and war, enemies, protection, initiation, and marriage.

- On Wednesdays, you should cast spells that involve communication and granting of information. Wednesday is governed by the planet Mercury and is represented by the deities Athena, Mercury, Hermes, Lugh, and Odin. It is also represented by the color purple, the metal mercury, and the gemstones agate and adventurine.

In addition, Wednesday is associated with aspen trees, ferns, lavenders, and lilies. It is also linked to traveling, journeys, loss and debt, and issues that are related to jobs and businesses.

- On Thursdays, you should cast spells for prosperity, success, and luck. Your spells will be more effective if you cast them during the waxing moon. Thursday is actually the best day for spell-casting because it is ruled by the planet Jupiter, which is generous and benevolent.

Thursday is represented by the deities Juno, Jupiter, Zeus, and Thor, as well as green and royal blue colors. It is also associated with tin, turquoise, lapis lazuli, and amethyst. Oak trees, honeysuckle, and cinquefoil are also best used during this day. Furthermore, Thursday is associated with family loyalty, honor, clothing and riches, and harvests.

- On Fridays, you should cast love spells and give offerings to your favorite gods and goddesses. Friday is governed by the planet Venus and the deities Freya, Aphrodite, and Venus. It is represented by copper, coral, rose quartz, and emerald. It is also represented by the colors pink and aqua.

During this day, feverfew, apple blossoms, and strawberries are best incorporated into spells. Friday is also associated with family life, fertility, sexuality, friendship, harmony, and growth so you may want to perform spells that revolve around these subjects.

- On Saturdays, you should cast banishing spells to get rid of old and negative energies. If you have to do a binding spell, you should do it on a Saturday because this day is most ideal for getting rid of unwanted energies and developing patience.

Saturday is ruled by the planet Saturn and is represented by the deities Saturn and Hecate. It is also represented by the colors black and dark purple, as well as lead, apache tear, hematite, and obsidian. Moreover, it is associated with thyme, cypress, and mullein. It is also linked to creativity, hope, fortune, protection, agriculture, and banishment of negativity.

Chapter 6:
Truth Spells on a Sunday

When Seeking for an Answer

If you are seeking answers from people with regard to something that they don't want to tell you, or you want to know the truth behind their lies, you can cast a truth spell. Here is a sample that you can use. For this truth spell, you will need a white candle, a blue candle, a needle, compelling oil, and five senses oil.

First, you have to carve the name of the person from which you are seeking an answer from on the white candle using the needle. Then, use the five senses oil to cover the white candle and the compelling oil to cover the blue candle. Light both candles and set them on a table. They should be several inches apart.

Focus your energy on the blue candle and recite the chant that you have made to seek the truth. You can come up with rhyming words about finding out the truth. Next, focus your attention on the white candle and say the name of the person whom you want to know the answer from.

Bring the two candles closer together slowly and recite another spell that makes your intentions of wanting to know the truth clear. Allow the candles to burn and wait for them to burn out. Afterwards, you should be able to obtain the truth that you wanted to obtain.

It's best to create your own spells. They can rhyme if you like, but this is not necessary. Simply create a short saying that expresses what you want the spell to achieve.

When Speaking with a Liar

On the other hand, if you feel that a person is lying to you, you can use this truth spell. You will need dried yellow roses, dried mint, nutmeg, a yellow candle, and olive oil. First, you have to coat the yellow candle with the olive oil until it becomes slick. In a container, mix the dried yellow roses, dried mint, and nutmeg.

Roll the candle into the mixture of herbs while thinking of your need to obtain the truth for clarity. Then, light the candle and recite your spell. Keep in mind that when casting a truth spell, you also become bound to speak the truth. So if you are also lying to the other person, your spell will not work.

Chapter 7:
Spells to Boost Confidence on a Monday

When doing a spell to boost confidence, you can use wild crystals, tree bark, wild herbs, and wild flowers. The ideal crystals to be used are amber, jet, azurite, and citrine. As for the wild herbs and flowers, you can use thyme, lavender, and bay laurel. In addition, you can use fragrant oils, candles, and blessed water. All of these elements can help you to increase your confidence and improve your ability to interact with other people.

Morning Confidence Spell

If you want a confidence spell that you can use in the morning, you should try this one out. You will need sandalwood incense and a red candle. Sandalwood incense is ideal due to its earthy scent. A red candle is crucial because it represents strength and power. You should perform the spell before you take a shower. Also, see to it that you speak slowly but loudly. Whispering the words and chants will not do.

Begin the spell by standing in front of a full-body mirror and lighting the candle. Focus your attention on the flame and work up your energy. You should feel positive energy starting to envelope your body. Do not rush the process. Working up your energy can take a few minutes. Once you have energized yourself, you should stare at your reflection in the mirror. Look into your own eyes and repeat your chant.

Tell yourself that you are intelligent and have the ability to succeed in anything that you set your mind to. Tell yourself that you will speak clearly and calmly, as well as only focus on the positive things. Tell yourself that you will not allow yourself to be shaken. Once again, remind yourself that you are intelligent and can succeed in any aspect of your life.

Visualize yourself beaming with self-pride and self-confidence. Imagine that you have finally gotten over your self-doubts. Light the incense and allow it to burn out while you get ready for the day.

Another Confidence Spell

This spell is effective done on a waxing moon, however is actually best performed on a new moon as it is during this time when the energies are high for bringing confidence. You will need a tiger's eye, but if you cannot get one, you can just use any gemstone that you have. You will also need a yellow candle, three white candles, and an optional rope or wire that you can use to turn the gemstone into a necklace.

To do the spell, go outside and stand under the moon. Arrange the three white candles into a triangle and place the yellow candle in the middle. Meditate and work up your energy while holding the tiger's eye. Make sure that you focus your energy into it. When you feel that you have composed yourself, light a white candle and recite your chant.

You can make up your own chant. It would be better if it rhymes. Nonetheless, you should request for the energies of the universe to give you the gifts of courage and strength. Then, light another white candle and repeat the chant. Light the final white candle and repeat the same chant. Lastly, light the yellow candle and hold the tiger's eye above its flame.

Recite your chant while you hold the tiger's eye. By the power of three, ask the energies of the universe to give you courage and strength. Stare at the flame and meditate. Imagine how you will feel once you have gained the confidence that you desire. Visualize yourself being calm and standing straight. Take several minutes to envision the whole thing while you send your energy into your gemstone.

Recite your final chant. It should be about charging the gemstone with light and love, as well as confidence and strength. By the power of three and the energies of the universe, ask for confidence and strength to be with you. When you are done with the chant, you can turn your gemstone into a necklace using the rope or the wire. If you do not want to wear it, you can simply keep it inside a small pouch. Recharge it anytime you need to.

Chapter 8:
A Protection Spell on a Tuesday

On a Tuesday, you can do this spell to keep you safe and protected against evil. You will need blue or silver glitter and your wand or staff. You actually need a blue, silver, or white wand. If your wand is of a different color, you can simply wrap it with a blue, silver, or white ribbon. Ideally, you should also perform this spell outdoors.

To do this spell, you should proceed with the steps of spell-casting as usual. However, instead of starting with the North, you should start with the West and move clockwise from there. Use your wand to tap the ground while you chant. Call upon to whoever guards the watchtowers of whichever direction you go to. Ask that you may be guided through the darkness and be safe at all times.

When you are done with the four corners, you should stand in the center and recite your chant. Your chant should be about banishing negative energies and never letting them come near you again. As you recite the last lines of your chant, scatter the glitter around you and close the circle to end the ritual.

Chapter 9:
A Spell to Improve Communication on a Wednesday

If you are having trouble communicating with someone or you feel that your lines of communication are weakening, you can cast a communication spell. You can use herbs such as chamomile to encourage understanding and communication. You can also use a pen with yellow ink since yellow is a color that is often associated with the element of air.

You need to write the name of the person you wish to communicate with on a white candle, preferably using a pen with yellow ink. Take some time to compose yourself and have an imaginary conversation with the person you wish to communicate with. Think of how you want your conversation to flow so you can send vibrations and energies.

When you are ready, you can recite your chant or spell. Ideally, you should ask the powers of the air to help you send your messages to that particular person.

Chapter 10:
A Money Spell on a Thursday

If you are having financial problems or you want to have more money, you should cast a money spell. However, you should take note that casting a money spell does not guarantee that you will become a millionaire.

Remember that casting a spell like this will only help you increase your chances of obtaining wealth and not actually make you instantly rich. In other words, you still have to exert effort if you want to make money.

Anyway, for this spell, you need to use lavender. Get a bag and put money in it. It should be seven different pieces. For instance, you can put in a nickel, a penny, a dime, a quarter, a dollar, and so on. Sprinkle your money liberally with lavender and carry the bag with you for seven days.

Chapter 11:
A Love Spell on a Friday

Are you looking for love? If you are, you should try this love spell. It is very short and quick to do. You will need a bottle of vanilla extract. See to it that you use a genuine vanilla extract and not an imitation.

Remove the lid of the bottle and imagine a bright red light coming from your eyes and turning the extract into the same red color. As you do this, you should recite your chant. It should be about bringing love into your life or about anything that you want to happen. Afterwards, you should sprinkle a drop or two of the extract in the four corners of your bedroom. Put back the lid on the bottle and keep it under your bed.

Chapter 12:
A Binding Spell on a Saturday

Binding spells are typically used to prevent something or someone from causing harm. Unlike curses, they do not inflict harm on another person. They are actually more like protection spells, except that they aim to get rid of the negative elements instead of simply wanting to be protected from it.

If you need a generic binding spell, you can do this one. You will need cardboard, black yarn, a cauldron, and writing tools. Get the cardboard and write words or draw images that represent the negativity that you wish to bind onto. Then, crumple the cardboard into a ball and wrap it with the black yarn.

You should wrap the yarn twenty-one times around the crumpled cardboard while chanting your spell. After this, you should tie the ends of the yarn into three sturdy knots. Finally, you should burn the yarn-wrapped cardboard inside your cauldron while you chant your final spell about getting rid of the negativity completely.

Once the words or images that represent negativity are burned, you should visualize things that represent positivity.

Conclusion

Thank you again for downloading this book!

I hope this book was able to help you learn more about Wicca and Wiccan spells!

The next step is to put this information to use, and begin using the power of Wiccan spells, and trying them out for yourself!

Finally, if you enjoyed this book, please take the time to share your thoughts and post a review on Amazon. It'd be greatly appreciated!

Thank you and good luck!

www.ingramcontent.com/pod-product-compliance
Lightning Source LLC
LaVergne TN
LVHW021745060526
838200LV00052B/3491